PERCUSSION

FILM FAVORITES

Solos and Band Arrangements
Correlated with Essential Elements® Band Method

Arranged by
MICHAEL SWEENEY, JOHN MOSS and PAUL LAVENDER

Welcome to ESSENTIAL ELEMENTS FILM FAVORITES! The arrangements in this versatile book can be used either in a full concert band setting or as solos for individual instruments. The SOLO pages appear at the beginning of the book, followed by the BAND ARRANGEMENT pages. The supplemental CD recording or PIANO ACCOMPANIMENT book may be used as an accompaniment for solo performance.

Percussion 1 Page	Percussion 2 Page	Title	Correlated with Essential Elements
2	3	Pirates Of The Caribbean	Book 1, page 24
4	5	My Heart Will Go On	Book 1, page 24
6	7	The Rainbow Connection	Book 1, page 24
8	9	May It Be	Book 1, page 34
10	11	You'll Be In My Heart	Book 1, page 34
12	13	Accidentally In Love	Book 2, page 15
14	15	Also Sprach Zarathustra	Book 2, page 15
16	17	Mission: Impossible Theme	Book 2, page 15
18	19	Music from Shrek	Book 2, page 32
20	21	Zorro's Theme	Book 2, page 32

ISBN 978-0-634-08705-9

HAL•LEONARD®
CORPORATION
7777 W. BLUEMOUND RD. P.O. BOX 13819 MILWAUKEE, WI 53213

00860155

From Walt Disney Pictures' PIRATES OF THE CARIBBEAN: THE CURSE OF THE BLACK PEARL

PIRATES OF THE CARIBBEAN

(A medley including: The Medallion Calls • The Black Pearl)

PERCUSSION 1
Snare Drum, Bass Drum

Music by KLAUS BADELT
Arranged by MICHAEL SWEENEY

PIRATES OF THE CARIBBEAN
(A medley including: The Medallion Calls • The Black Pearl)

PERCUSSION 2
Sus. Cym., Small Tom

Music by KLAUS BADELT
Arranged by MICHAEL SWEENEY

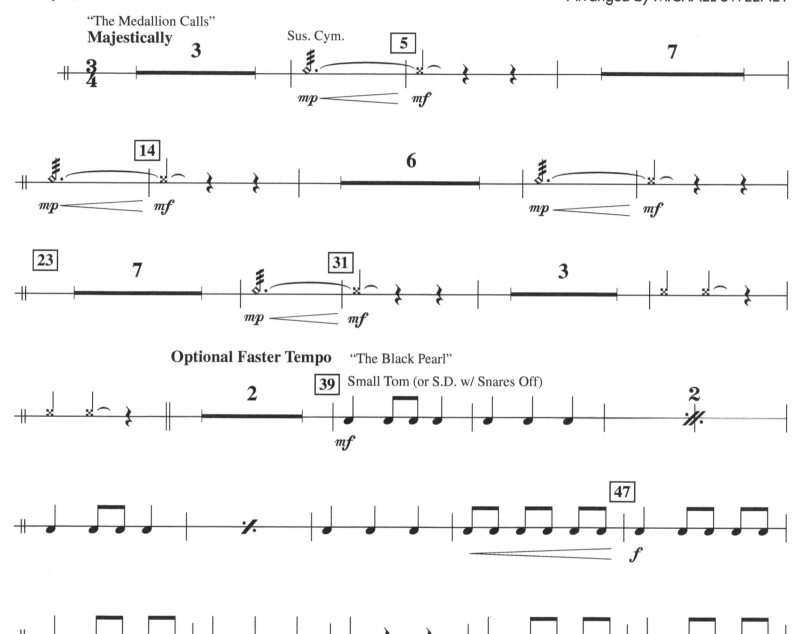

00860155

From the Paramount and Twentieth Century Fox Motion Picture TITANIC

MY HEART WILL GO ON
(Love Theme From 'Titanic')

PERCUSSION 1
Sus. Cym., Snare Drum, Bass Drum

Music by JAMES HORNER
Lyric by WILL JENNINGS
Arranged by JOHN MOSS

From the Paramount and Twentieth Century Fox Motion Picture TITANIC

MY HEART WILL GO ON

(Love Theme From 'Titanic')

Music by JAMES HORNER
Lyric by WILL JENNINGS
Arranged by JOHN MOSS

PERCUSSION 2
Triangle, Wind Chimes,
Cabasa, Sus. Cym.

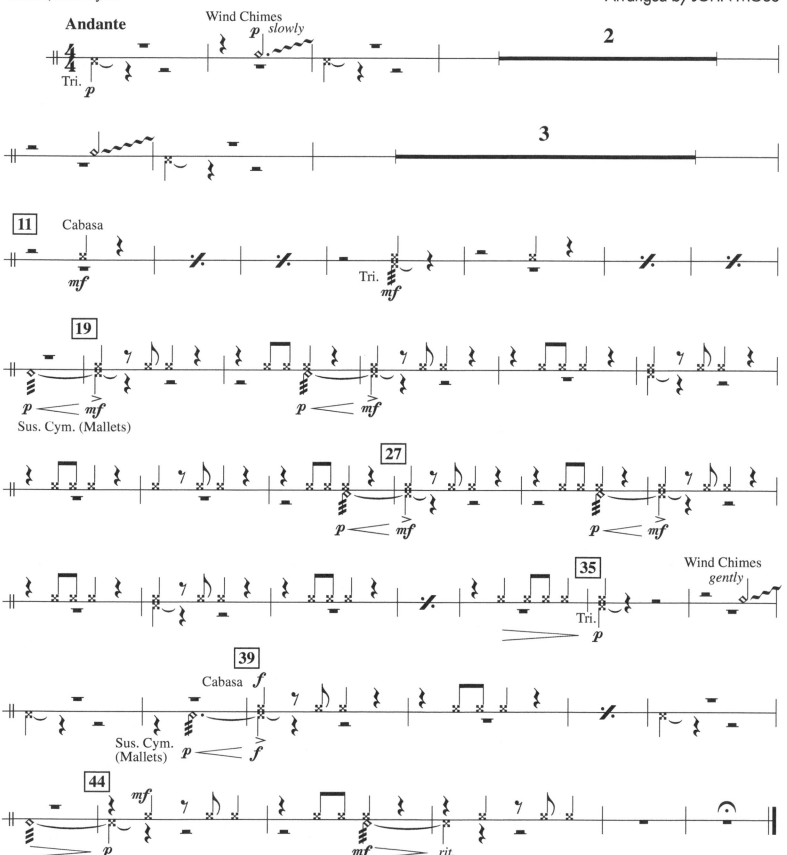

00860155

From THE MUPPET MOVIE

THE RAINBOW CONNECTION

PERCUSSION 1
Snare Drum, Bass Drum

Words and Music by
PAUL WILLIAMS and KENNETH L. ASCHER
Arranged by PAUL LAVENDER

From THE MUPPET MOVIE
THE RAINBOW CONNECTION

PERCUSSION 2
Triangle, Sus. Cym.

Words and Music by
PAUL WILLIAMS and **KENNETH L. ASCHER**
Arranged by PAUL LAVENDER

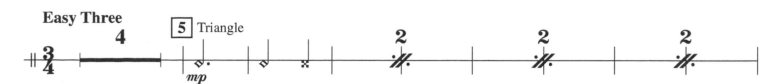

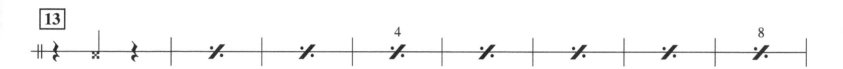

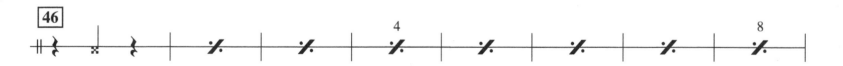

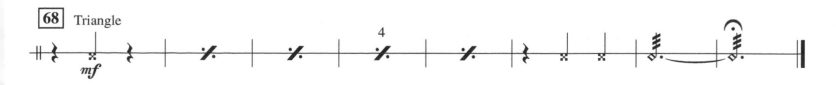

00860155

From THE LORD OF THE RINGS: THE FELLOWSHIP OF THE RING

MAY IT BE

PERCUSSION 1
Snare Drum, Bass Drum

**Words and Music by EITHNE NI BHRAONAIN,
NICKY RYAN and ROMA RYAN**
Arranged by JOHN MOSS

MAY IT BE

PERCUSSION 2
Wind Chimes, Triangle, Sus. Cym., Ride Cym.

**Words and Music by EITHNE NI BHRAONAIN,
NICKY RYAN and ROMA RYAN**
Arranged by JOHN MOSS

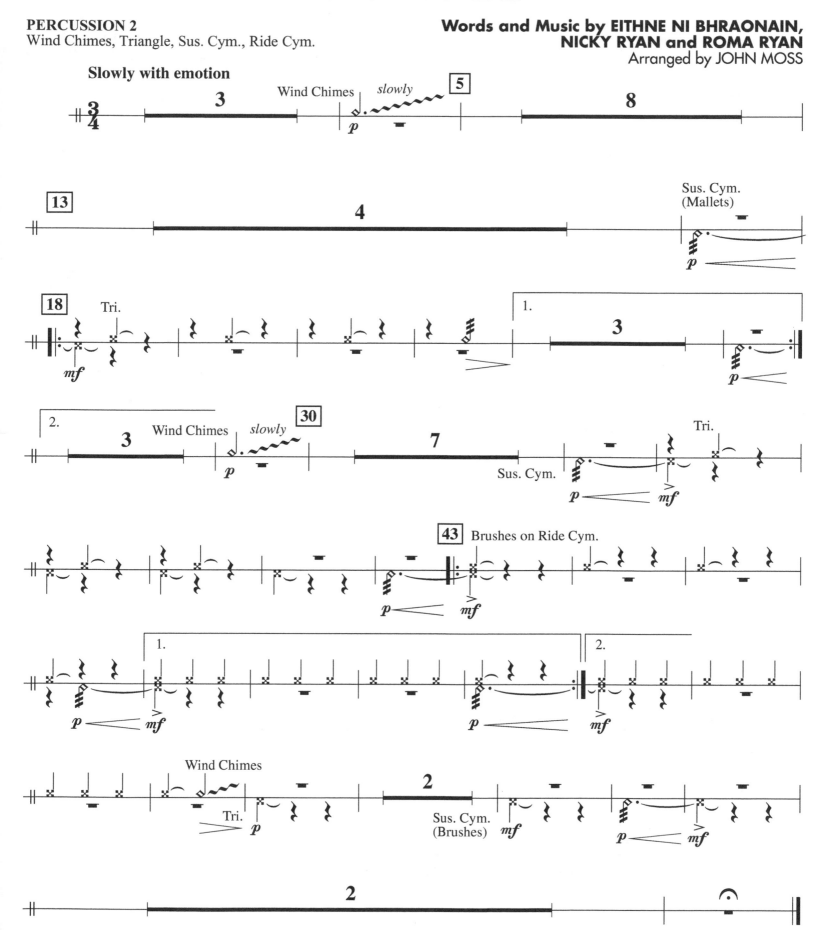

From Walt Disney Pictures' TARZAN™

YOU'LL BE IN MY HEART

PERCUSSION 1
African Hand Drum or Snare Drum,
Bass Drum or Djembe

Words and Music by
PHIL COLLINS
Arranged by MICHAEL SWEENEY

00860155

From Walt Disney Pictures' TARZAN™
YOU'LL BE IN MY HEART

PERCUSSION 2
Wind Chimes, Sus. Cym.,
Rain Stick, Shaker

**Words and Music by
PHIL COLLINS**
Arranged by MICHAEL SWEENEY

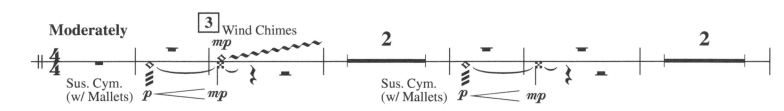

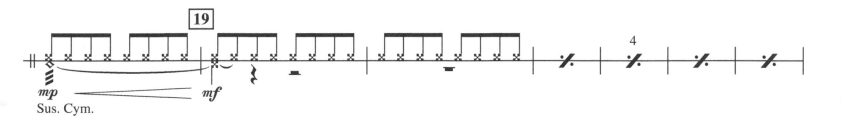

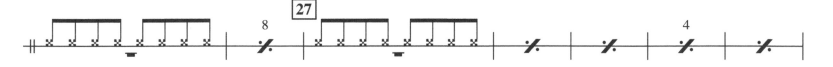

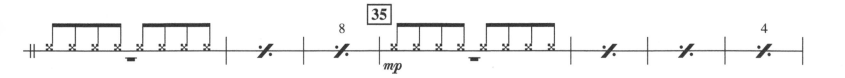

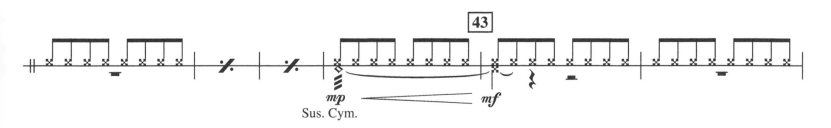

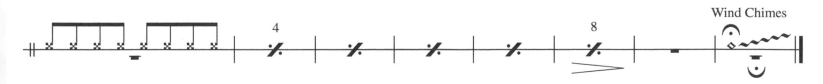

00860155

From the Motion Picture SHREK 2

ACCIDENTALLY IN LOVE

PERCUSSION 1
Opt. Drum Set

Words and Music by
ADAM F. DURITZ
Arranged by MICHAEL SWEENEY

00860155

From the Motion Picture SHREK 2

ACCIDENTALLY IN LOVE

PERCUSSION 2
Tambourine

Words and Music by
ADAM F. DURITZ
Arranged by MICHAEL SWEENEY

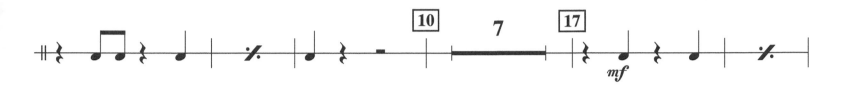

Featured in the Motion Picture 2001: A SPACE ODYSSEY

ALSO SPRACH ZARATHUSTRA

By RICHARD STRAUSS
Arranged by MICHAEL SWEENEY

PERCUSSION 1
Snare Drum, Bass Drum

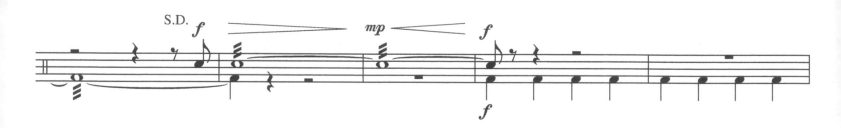

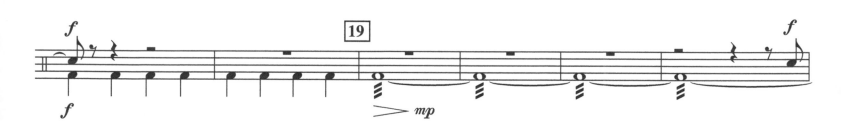

00860155

ALSO SPRACH ZARATHUSTRA

By RICHARD STRAUSS
Arranged by MICHAEL SWEENEY

PERCUSSION 2
Cr. Cym., Sus. Cym.

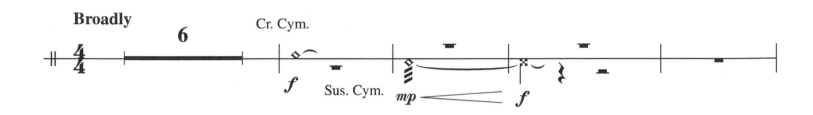

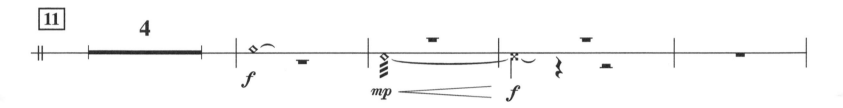

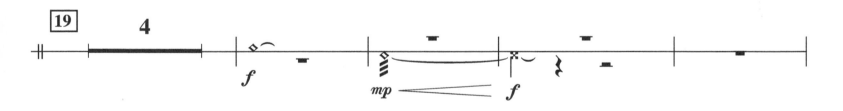

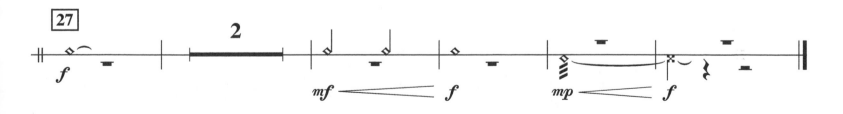

00860155

From the Paramount Motion Picture MISSION: IMPOSSIBLE

MISSION: IMPOSSIBLE THEME

PERCUSSION 1
Ride Cym., S.D., B.D., H.H.
(Opt. Drum Set)

By LALO SCHIFRIN
Arranged by MICHAEL SWEENEY

MISSION: IMPOSSIBLE THEME

PERCUSSION 2
Bongos

By LALO SCHIFRIN
Arranged by MICHAEL SWEENEY

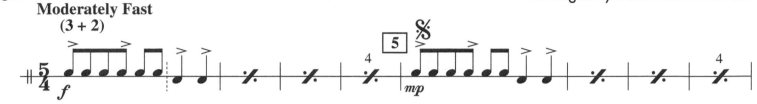

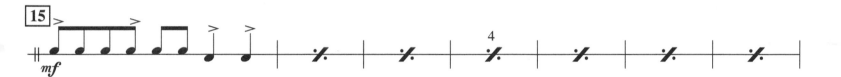

From SHREK
MUSIC FROM SHREK
(A medley including: Fairytale Opening • Ride The Dragon)

PERCUSSION 1
Snare Drum, Bass Drum

Music by JOHN POWELL and HARRY GREGSON-WILLIAMS
Arranged by JOHN MOSS

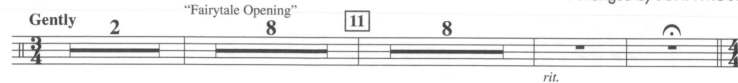

From SHREK

MUSIC FROM SHREK

(A medley including: Fairytale Opening • Ride The Dragon)

PERCUSSION 2
Triangle, Tamb., Sus. Cym., Cr. Cym.

Music by JOHN POWELL and HARRY GREGSON-WILLIAMS
Arranged by JOHN MOSS

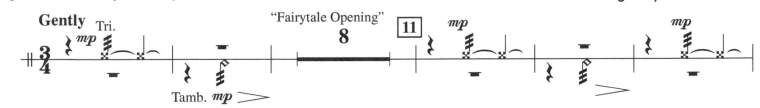

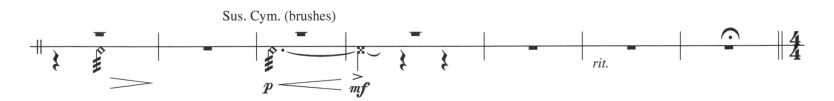

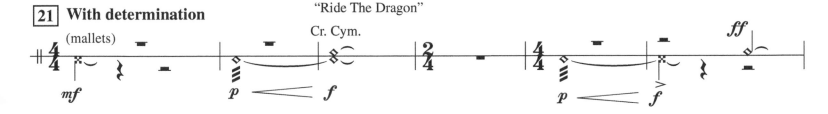

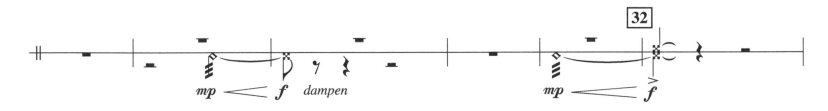

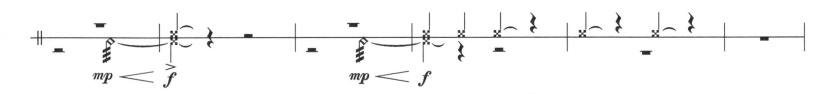

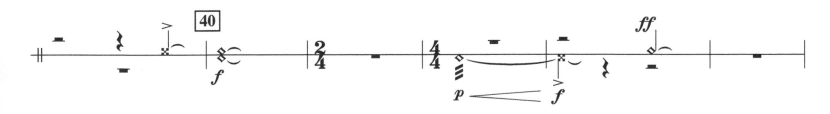

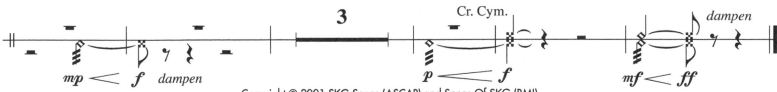

From the TriStar Motion Picture THE MASK OF ZORRO

ZORRO'S THEME

PERCUSSION 1
Snare Drum, Bass Drum

Composed by JAMES HORNER
Arranged by JOHN MOSS

Heroically

S.D. (Brushes)

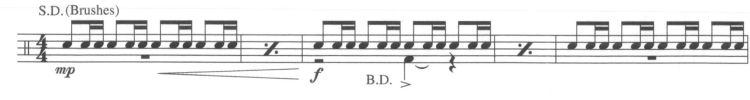

From the TriStar Motion Picture THE MASK OF ZORRO

ZORRO'S THEME

PERCUSSION 2
Cabasa, Sus. Cym., Maracas

Composed by JAMES HORNER
Arranged by JOHN MOSS

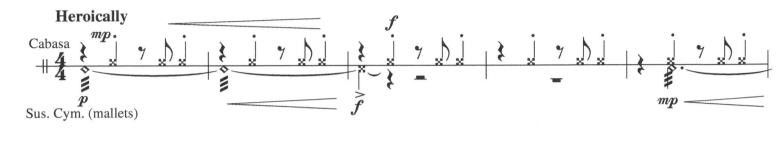

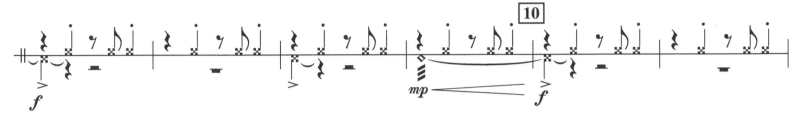

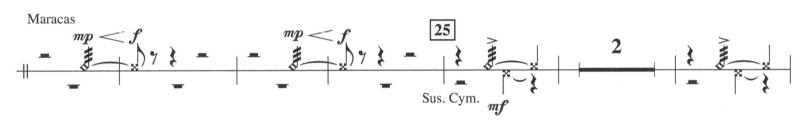

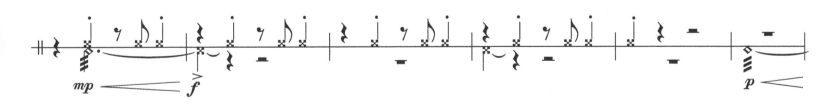

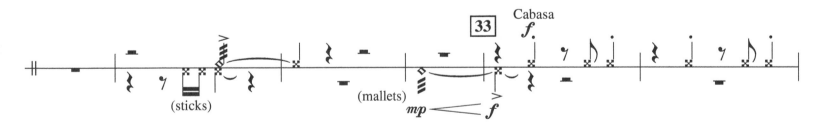

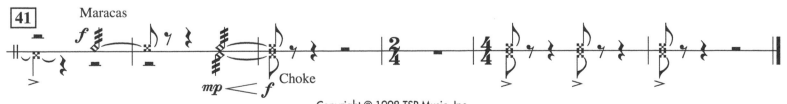